Words We Leave Behind

poetry and lyrics by

MARTIN FAWKES

oceandeep
P R E S S

Interior artwork adapted from "St. Albans Starlight"
by Chris Fawkes © www.chrisfawkes.com

WORLDS
  WE
    LEAVE
      BEHIND

ISBN 978-0-6456419-0-5

Published by
OCEANDEEP
PO Box 4264
Geelong VIC 3220 Australia
www.oceandeep.com.au

Poetry is just the evidence of life.
If your life is burning well,
poetry is just the ash.

Leonard Cohen

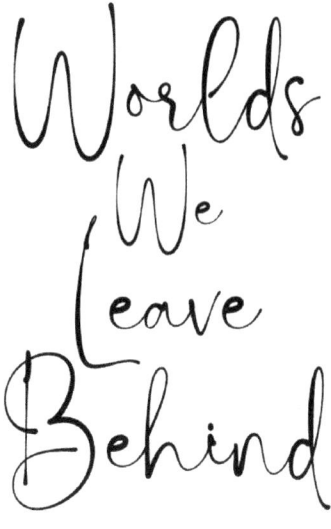

Worlds We Leave Behind

poetry and lyrics by

MARTIN FAWKES

oceandeep
PRESS

CONTENTS

PART THREE: A DREAM OF FLIGHT

A Beginning: The Distance ❋ Aces Continuing ❋ Beg For Breaking ❋ Blankless ❋ Bright (Yes, but Does It Have Teeth?) ❋ Choir of Angles ❋ Cleaners ❋ Dance With Me ❋ Deep ❋ Delirium and After ❋ Don't Do That, Do That ❋ The Dramas ❋ Eve ❋ Every Shade of Grace ❋ Every Word ❋ Far Enough ❋ Fell ❋ The First Denial

PART TWO: OFF TO THE RACES

Flag and Radar ❋ Forget ❋ Get Free ❋ The Glamour ❋ Gone to Hello ❋ Good but Gone ❋ Hallway Heels ❋ Happiness ❋ I Won the War ❋ If That's News ❋ In Tatters ❋ Knots ❋ Last Reveal ❋ Light My Days ❋ Little ❋ Lost Us in the Undertow ❋ Lost Your Hold ❋ Making It Up on the Spur of the Moment ❋ Mapwise

PART ONE: THE RAILS, ON & OFF

Match This ❋ The Melt ❋ Necessary Tarmac - Look Away ❋ Never Loved ❋ Night of the Living Deadline ❋ No Doubt (Goodbye Yesterdays) ❋ Noisier ❋ Nothing Ironic ❋ Nothing Left ❋ Numb ❋ On My Mind ❋ Only Remember ❋ Otherwise ❋ Oxygen ❋ Plus ❋ Poem on Demand ❋ Remembering

PART ZERO: AD ASTRA, TO THE STARS

Remind Me ❋ Reveal ❋ Sky ❋ So It's Happy ❋ Something New ❋ Sound and Fury (Grind) ❋ The Steps ❋ Those Waves ❋ Voice ❋ Wait ❋ Well ❋ What We Knew ❋ What We Knew Now ❋ Winter's Gone ❋ The World As We Didn't Know It ❋ Vespers – Goodnight

Here are the poetic stories of longing and loss.

Love, laughter and all that remains.

Resilience, imagination, ambition, achievement.

Hubris, failure, turmoil, stillness, calmness.

The agreements that keep us civil, the kindnesses that keep us sane.

Speaking into the void, feeling heard and unheard.

The disagreements, departures and arrivals that bring us anger, clarity, bliss.

Works of connection, disconnection, reconnection, courage, hunger, renewal.

The leaps of faith into the abyss, spontaneity, hope, doubt, death and rebirth.

The joys of friendship, remembering, hiding and being found, none too early, never too late, misunderstandings and new understandings.

Knowledge and innocence, wisdom, wellness, freedom and consequence, promises kept and lost, emptiness and fulfilment.

Welcome to Worlds We Leave Behind!

a dream of flight

A BEGINNING: THE DISTANCE

One more sip of coffee now
Before you go
A wing across the world
Some prearranged small daydream
For you girl
A glimmer less of knowing
Than of hope
Let distance unravel getting
Sparkled once but soon forgetting

And who can call the timing of us now?
Decide apart these human hearts somehow
Too smart to think so simply
What did you mean to me?
Unfog my shaded eyes
And help me see

So drain your cup or glass
Wherever you are
Somewhere or other in the world
Weave together fraying strands
A garment new
Not made with hands
The distance fades or firms the knowing
What was staying once is going
Now it's going
Now it's going

ACES CONTINUING

Whack! Yellow sphere reappears
Before your noisy racket
Smack! return, impaction, friction
Smart reaction, stretch and take the necessary action
Further grin and gurn let otherside burn
Perspiring, fatigue can bite it all it likes
Bitumen meant it every minute
Got to burn it
Got to win it
Got a purse
Enormous purse
To earn

BEG FOR BREAKING

I can do this all day
So you say
You're not a horse, workhorse, so to contradict
I might abstain from saying
Nay, nevertheless, the stress, under duress,
Whirlwind spins, can you stand still
Long, long enough
to avoid becoming your own cliché?

A draught horse will pull a plow
Across a field, so far so good
But cannot take the land
Which side of the Jordan do you want, now?
Do you understand?
Do not break and stay so broken
It's ok to time-away, repair, be strong again
and stand

Don't have to beg for breaking
Life itself will take you there
In good time, of its own accord
Quick or slow, soon or tomorrow
Who is going to remake you though?
Time, make time
Grab time by the horns if you have to
Time to take the break, brake, unbreak
Be whole
And GO

BLANKLESS

The first stroke of ink
Dark splatter sparks some chatter
Did you ever stop to think
Any little thing you did
didn't matter
It all connects to something
Impacts to something
Changes something
Act, react, impact
Something's different now
That's a fact
Let's make a pact to keep
At it, face up to all the
Thought that sidelines
Count for naught, we ought
To say or do anything instead
Of watching only
Splat the page with blue or black
Each stroke of ink speaks
Out for something
Something new
New now, reach into
The void, undo the
Blank

BRIGHT (YES, BUT DOES IT HAVE TEETH?)

Simple murmurs in your ear
A good idea is a good idea
Lightbulb moment sneaks up
like a sneaky thing
An electric shock of fresh cognition
ignition of the new
Sinews tense, untense, elate
inflate, intensive moment
Wicks alight, fuses cooled
sparks are struck
Good luck, frisson and friction
might create a flame
A new notion is better than a circle
walked once too often
A certain surplus of heat
I might admire
Don't close your eyes, delighted by
the less than blinding waves
Go on
Go surf those rays

CHOIR OF ANGLES

Obtuse? Oh, funny you should say
That as I never quite saw it that way
Not inclined to strictly observe, always
Preferred the slightly wayward swerve
Except in hind
Sight, I might realise, now open up
My eyes upon looking
Back at that slighting, sledging, backhanded
Deadening wind-up, closure not taking the mick, if you get
my drift, shudder and sway, subtle moving away
From all you had, you're holding tightly
In my visualizing, so unsightly, unbecoming
Something less than what you were, don't strangle
It with a vice-like grip
You could have been a world, but now little
less than a neighbourhood
Ah, what could
Have been, ride up the ramp
Defy the gravity if you can
What's on the other side of this hill-traversing ride
Get over it, beyond the rampant climb
Didn't take a saboteur to bring it all
Undone, just a little inattention where it mattered
You could have been a world, but now little
less than a neighbourhood
Too much introspection where not required
Shatter now, a call to fall together
Don't draw the lines
We'll have to see you by the time
You get there, to the other side
For all the sudden fall, I still enjoyed
The ride

CLEANERS

They took me to the cleaners
They had hung me out to dry
They thought they had me pegged
and perhaps I'd egged them on
and who knows why?

I have a bright and sparkling future
Hanging in some part of town
I know-not-where
I got the ticket in my jacket pocket
Some sort of docket to redeem
The silver lining that is my soul

New clothes and new shoes
Nothing now that's left to lose
It's no longer on the line
It's mine

They thought they'd wipe me out
But I run deeper than their schemes
And the end they thought they'd bring me
Ain't as final as it seemed
It's just the beginning
Come to nothing all you nothings
There's such a something left of me
Cos' I am FREE

DANCE WITH ME

The day I saw your silhouette
A hint of laughter on your lips
I caught a glimpse, the light
of who you are

A twirl, a sway, a pirouette
A loveliness I won't forget
To take your hand and then
to hold you near

O sublime vision in a dress
The gentleness of your caress...
Come dance with me
Come dance with me

It was a day without regret
Contagious smile for our duet
To twirl and spin and sway
With you always

Sublime vision in a dress
The gentleness of your caress...
Come dance with me
Come dance with me

So come on, fall into my arms
Surrender to whatever charms
I own or lack
We're going back now
to square one
At last we have begun
To dance!

DEEP

How deep, how still
These are truths
I need to know
Come knit them in my bones

If I climbed the highest high
Reached right up, pulled down the sky
Would I fall back down
Back down to earth
If I descend the deepest sea
Would the pressure be the end of me
Feel the coldness and
the ache deep deep inside my skin
An end is a beginning, of a kind
How far from cloud to ocean floor
Measure once, and grab your saw
Cut to the chase and ask what for
To travel all that way
So far, so deep, so still
So, still I ask
Come knit
into my bones, all these
deep truths I still
still need
still need
still need
to know

DELIRIUM AND AFTER

"There's nothing to it!"
These are not
The first words said
Inside, the first words you tell
yourself
Perhaps the third, or second
things to think
As you strain to train yourself
in self-hypnosis
And up-talk: "I can do anything"
"can do anything"
"do anything"
"anything!"
As your life spirals
Feet first
Into the firmament

DON'T DO THAT, DO THAT

He stopped you on the way to the door
"A word", he arched an eyebrow
in your general direction
You caught one or two of those heavy-brows
once or twice before
"Why stop at one?" would have been
all the reply he's owed
If you cared to query
what's the theory behind those dark-eyed glares

"Any word?" she asked, not vainly
When he'd plainly been unable to gather just
one wit about what's stable and disorderly
around the plans they'd planned to make
but not begun

"why not" he sighed, beguiling
crafty smiling, gathering wool
thinking, laughing, after all, what matters most
Is written, signed
at least in your mind
"Don't worry now" he reassured
"It's all in hand, under control, sorted, above board"
All threats of debts remain in custody
Parole in 90 days or so
Don't worry, just be ready to arrest your expectations
Don't panic, there's no overload suspected
Just a little bit of forward motion

No problem, then, a little wine
A little food, dessert and all
A little smile, look out
We're gonna be here for a while

THE DRAMAS

Do not bring your lowly dramas
While still wrapped in your pyjamas
If you're going to get excited
Make it something big
Worth getting ignited for

So the price is slightly wrong on something
Pay the price or begin discussing
But fight? Why elevate the hackles
Make sure the outcome is worth the battles
Moderate the verbal motion
Captivate the right emotion
Raise your voice for proper cause
Otherwise put shouts on pause

Do not bring up your lowly dramas
While still wrapped in your emotional pyjamas
If you're going to get excited
Make it something big
Something really worth igniting for

EVE

Furtive spritz
Of not quite sunshine
Sunful day near twilight
Turns to grey
Deposits of tranquillity and calm
For mine, that's all I'd ask
To task a balmy early springtime eve
Every pleasant solitary time
One deep breath and all is fine

EVERY SHADE OF GRACE

I'm gonna need better glasses
If I'm going to be
Held to account for all there is
I ought to see

For if the sun also rises
and the rain also falls
If I sleep the sleep of the just
I must give thanks for the mercy after all

EVERY WORD

Every situation finds an action
or reaction needed
Every little crisis makes a canyon or it builds
a bridge
And every little word I've used
has been in place
to build you up
I'd not replace a one
They've all been put right there
with every care and meaning
Hope and faith don't need replacing
Written, said, unspoken
Every little phrase or thought
expressed, invested, spent all spent
without regret, and meant
So little there to change
Sincerely yours
they are yours
to keep
or put away
But still I meant it all
I meant
every word
I had to say

FAR ENOUGH

The burr of soft acceleration
Sighing, subtle braking down the incline
As the tunnel beckons
Traffic banked as far as I can see
These metal beetles crawling slow
And still, it seems, so far to go
To be as far as far away needs to be

So soon
Soon enough
I will be home
Home
But until then
I'm not far enough away

The bite of tyred gravel
Crackles darkly in those rims
And cold winds beckon forth the shiverings
Old friends to find and nourish
If they've braved the traveling
To find the life between dark whispers
Flint a spark across the distance

Home
Soon enough
I will be home
But until then
I'm not far enough away

FELL

I fell from a great height
But I hit the ground running
I awoke in fright
With no insight forthcoming

I sent for the jesters
Trustworthy investors
Dislike and detestors
The glibness infesting
The rest of the questions
Which way now?
Who could say?

THE FIRST DENIAL

The first denial – they shut up shop
Nowhere to be found
At least not in the usual location
Can't argue with that
Have to get my soup elsewhere
The second denial – too many staff
Cleaning, taking a break
or finishing their shift
to serve any customers
I'm third in line, I'll give them three minutes
Er, no I won't
The third denial – ads everywhere
For the newest, the greatest
The mouthwateringliest deliciousest
but 'sorry, we stopped serving those 15 minutes ago
oh, (as an apology) the ice cream is still good!
Great! But I can't read the prices without my glasses
So I wander to another vendor (again)
and cope with a mediocre cupcake
and barely passable coffee

off to the races

FLAG AND RADAR

The flag you planted firmly I did not salute
Not for lack of respect
I was simply looking, watching, listening
Inhaling to glean some understanding
Attentive to the minutiae
Antennae trying to tune in
to your wavelength

If I observe an undercurrent of anxious
A breeze of unease
Or a small hint of uncertain, let me reassure
All the many plans I've calculated, incubated
Did not include disappearing, no puffs of smoke
No seeking applause or final curtain
There is no audience for what we have going on
Just a handful of non-observers
So keep on speaking, I'll keep adjusting my radar
Blips on my screen, what is your heart saying?
What can I do to decompress the tension
f your pressing situation?

FORGET

The sullen tides of memory
Throw their chains around these feet
Rankling, dragging
Precious artifacts of personal history
To hide and bury in the seas

And all the mustering of will
Cannot descend to view
Every facet of those jewels
That are my memories of you

Ageless faces, conversations
Places, dim outlines of all we knew
Still I remember
Still I remember you

GET FREE

Couldn't cash in the moment
Couldn't franchise the opportunity
Call the stars as my witness
And the gossip columnists
To the getting
To the getting of me
It costs so much
Costs so much
This thing called get free

THE GLAMOUR

I'll take the glamour if it's all you've got
But where's the human skin beneath the sculpt
The dazzling lights blaze broadly for the great unwashed
Is there's luminescence here not wrought by halogen?

You want to unscrew the unscrupulous
Undo the inscrutable
Sense the insensible
Unmute the immutable

I don't know if you can, my man
Don't know if that's a good idea, my dear
Can you see the horizon from here?
Decline the overshine
Simply be yourself

I'll supercede the superficial
For the thoughtless thought
Is there a human being behind
What comes to next to naught
The dazzling lights can burn the skin
But not illuminate the shadow

Do you wanna scrape the unscrupulous
Unscrew the inscrutable
Sense the insatiable
Unmute the immutable

I don't know if you can, my man
Don't know if that's a good idea, my dear
Can you see the horizon from over here?
Decline the overshine
Simply be yourself
Decline the overshine
If you're so inclined
Simply be yourself

GONE TO HELLO

So much fear attached to the notion
That someone might be wrong
Send them to a pit they don't recognise
Maybe that will open up their eyes
No sense of turning the other cheek
When you could smite them, better yet
Just go to hell, oh, why not yet
Their sordid senses of forgiven-ness
What for is it even given
Good gracious, can't show kindness
Towards the heretics
Let burning coals be literal and actual
Forgo the figures of speech
Once those foes presided well
But now somehow
Forgetting all the goodness
Mutually imparted
Old friendships wrangled, mangled,
Dismantled, overreached
Breached
What is that sulphuric smell?
The stench of silly fear, I fear
Drawn near

GOOD BUT GONE

Here we are again
Tear it up again
Looking at the faces, places
Where we will not go (or be, or know) again
Don't be shy
When it's time
To say
Good

Good and so it was
Good and so it was
Good
And so it was good
And so it was good
Now it's good-bye!

HALLWAY HEELS

The clatter of her shoes
Announce her imminent arrival
At least a good 45 seconds
Before I see her face
So sorry I'm late? Don't be silly
You're right on time!

HAPPINESS

A little less than helpless
A fair bit more than morbid
A little lower
Than understanding
Can I be more of a man
And not so demanding

Is it happy yet?
Is it happy yet?
So hard to pin down my happiness

More rested than underestimated
Far flatter than
the story was inflated
More invested than revealed
When it's all investigated
What more can I stand?
How do I help you understand?

Is it happy yet?
Is it happy yet?
So hard to pin down my happiness

Is it happy yet?
Trying to pin it down
Happy yet?
The word within
Happy?
App reboot install stall it intuit into it
Happiness is it gonna visit yes
Oh yes

I WON THE WAR

Sometimes it felt like chess
At others like ballet
Sometimes we looked too close
Sometimes we looked the other way
Sometimes it seemed like a house on fire
Sometimes we had to wait for the choir
Adoring voices, rising, take us higher
I looked you in the eye as we said aye
I won the war
I won the war that day

Later, some legislated moments of distress
Handed down and turned around
The point I made, replying, somehow did not impress
Such simple words left a gaping wound
Right there inside your chest
I won the war
I won the war but lost a world that day

Sometimes we'd speak so loud until
No words were there to say
What is left when there's nothing left
Do you speak out anyway?
Anything I had would be out of turn
According to your newly turned out rulings
Tabled in my intray ixnay isspay au fait
Leading by the nose isn't really leading
Was I pleading for some sense?
Don't be dense, just fade away
You looked me in the eye, dared me to move
So I did and walked
I won the war, I won the war
I won the war when I walked away

IF THAT'S NEWS

Your kindness and attention lifted my game
Your generosity and lightness of heart, the same
And for all your uncertainties and nervous edge
You looked me in the eye like I was a human being
not a number or a stereotype
You did indeed lean on me, eventually
to get certain things done in certain ways
But maybe it was the places where you weren't quite looking
changed the most
You made me happy for awhile
You calmed me down and helped me still
an inner cyclone or two
You could do that
And you did

I'm sorry
So very sorry
If nobody ever told you
So sorry if that's news

For all the inner aching
I can see now, from a distance
While we were close I was thankful
For your kindness and generosity
For the intrepid soul I saw
And I'm sorry
So very sorry
If nobody ever told you
So sorry if that's news
So sorry noone told you that before

IN TATTERS

So all the seasons wrapping is in tatters
Never mind all that, too late too bad
It's the thought, after all, that matters
Heart in the right place
Never mind the fray
Never mind how it looks
This unglamorous lump won't get on network TV now
The lights are down, this is all a bit off script
Reality wasn't meant to be this "real" now, was it?
Now the sun is setting and Arcturus
still ascendant in the sky
There are floaty, glowey dudes out in the fields, up high
What on earth does all this mean?

It's all the heart, after all, that matters
What is seen is not only how it is, you know
How can a newborn, lying helpless
Help express
All the creative anguish, joy and soon-come sorrow
Wipe the slate, clean our clocks, wash our plate
Of all the uneaten, undigested leftovers of neglect
That our unfocused, unwilling, easily distracted hearts
have left
Not just a law to make us tidy up our room
Here is a child, a broom
Boom

So all my excuses are in tatters
Nothing left to say, except "Father, please forgive"
My hands are almost empty now
No good thing left to bring
Except what you have made of me

So where is it?
Where is my promised joy?
I want my promise, today
And yesterday
And always
Where is my promised joy?
Ah, a gift, at last I see it all
Wrapped up in a baby boy

KNOTS

I not stand for falling down
I not run for standing still
I not stay for move away
Make of this what you will

I not sleep for stay awake
I not yell for ears that break
I not tell you what remains
Do not worry, just be safe

There is not a day goes by
I don't wanna look you in the eye
And say... something
Something, something

LAST REVEAL

The one thing
Only
I never wanted known
You never quite knew
Before
It's true

The second thing
Of many
I could care to not have shown
Did you know that? Did I say that?
Is it true?

Thirdly, have I mentioned
Anything about intentions
To disclose?
Who, who knows?

To know thyself is wondrous space
To perceive yourself and know your place
Behind, beyond, before
Sometimes the words
of another, needed
Spoken fitly
To reframe
What it's all for

LIGHT MY DAYS

I'm not gonna plead now
And I never thought you wanted that, anyhow
I'm just gonna ask nice, once or twice
Put your hand on my heart
And help me be calm, becalm me
Calm me if you please
Keep my heart at ease

      And if you see a shadow on my brow
      Light my days
      Cast the mist away
      Light my days
      Light my days
      Light my days

I'm not gonna plead now
I never thought that was the way to go
Sometimes I went there anyway
But we know better, know each other better
Than that melodrama sideshow
Just walk beside me if you will
And I'll keep your hand in mine
We'll be just fine, just fine
Just fine

      And if you see a shadow in my soul
      Light my days
      Cast the uncalm trouble all away
      Light my days
      Light my days
      Light my days

LITTLE

Little King
Of all you survey
Perhaps some one
Some thing
Will open up your eyes
To what is real
One day

LOST US IN THE UNDERTOW

Every word we spoke in jest
Like a thump inside your chest
Unwilling withdrawal, not invested
At all, at all in their best interest
Every thing we overthrow
Could turn out to lose us in the undertow
Still we put it out there
Still we put it out there, hoping
Every tune we overthrow
Could turn out lost inside the undertow
Still we put it out there
Still we put it out there, hoping
Someone's listening

LOST YOUR HOLD

For what it's worth, the price invested
That small return, half-interested
The tuning out, the poor reception
The shrugging off, the half-exception

This ain't digital television
Bright pixelation
Uninterrupted vision

The monstrosity
In the corner of the room
Ain't even elephantine
Your set is broke
Lost hold
Lost hold, vertical glitch
You'll need to stitch it all up quick

For all the view uninterrupted
Feast your eyes but brains corrupted
Hypnotised by endless repetition
So much seeing, so little vision

That screen
In the corner of the room
Ain't even elephantine
Your set is broke
Lost hold
Lost hold
Lost hold

MAKING IT UP ON THE SPUR OF THE MOMENT

Improvise, extemporise
Grab a word or two, a groove
and move!
Whatever tools lie to hand
A turn of phrase, semiquavers
Melodies
A gentle violence if
we overfill everyspace
with disrespect to silence
Any moment now I'll have to stop
In case this improv
Sounds much less like jazz
And too much like hip-hop

Whatever's to hand, conjugations
Adjectivals, nouns and verbs
Rearrange their situations, structures sounding
Strange, thoughtful or absurd
Perhaps a dis- or re-connect of
What is said and what is heard

MAPWISE

See, it wasn't all that far from there to here
Just a minute for a lifetime
Just an hour for all these years
And all I have to show for it is just this guitar right here
And all the memories
If I could remember these
Just memories

See, it wasn't all that hard to travel far to near
Just waited while the going
Propelled me through the laughs and tears
And all I have to show now are the clothes upon my back
Not much, but not for nothing will I lack
If I could remember anything
I will remember these
These simple memories

See, the hardest thing to face
Was running straight between the lines
A destination lacking detailed maps with no surprise
A thatway over yonder, go to upside of downunder
Sleep above the fishes sometime
Disembark before the downtime
Twilight zombie 'til the morning
One day's new day begins dawning
When you open up your eyes
And all I have to show for it
Is this guitar right here
And all the memories
And all the memories
If I remember these
I remember these

ONE

The rails, off and on

MATCH THIS

Scritch and scratch, to scrape a match
A puff of sulphur, smoke, then fire
Three seconds worth of flame
And then, if nothing else
The world is dark again
Without a friend
Without a friend
Without a friend to take the burden

When cold winds blow and draughts chill bones
One by one the lights can dim
When fear rules minds
Turbulent times
When trust is dissed
And kindness missed
When strangers seem more like strange
And less like friends we haven't met
Worry and fear takes hold of hearts
That ought be much brighter yet
So ease that worldly chill
Come, start that fire
If all you have is just little itch
To make a difference
It only takes a tiny match
Hold it thus, a little scratch
Pass on the flame you get to start
And warm the next cool heart

So take the light
And pass along the fire
What lights your wick
and warms your wax
When all the light is lacking?
Slow combustion
Strike a light and spread the flame
Come, warm a worried world again
With a friend
With a friend
With friends to share the burden
Hope again

THE MELT

Long ago first waiting for the thaw
Summer gone away for good
But goodness knows some follies
are worth waiting for
No sense remaining in the small circle
I once thought of as my world
So here am I outside again
still waiting for my girl

The ice it shut me out from you
so long ago
Excluded from your love by all that
frost and snow
It wasn't always the way this way, as you
so clearly know
What will reach beneath the sheets of cold
Disrupt the layers of deep freezing
Return it all to fluid motion
Simple patience and devotion never seemed to
reach you
And if I never told you
what would you know?

NECESSARY TARMAC - LOOK AWAY

Certain things I could feel
But not allowed to express
Without a valve to release
How can I decompress
So much pressure building up
Something certain gonna burst
And if it's you who isn't listening
Then it's me who'll come off worst
You gave your shortsighted disciple
The keys to the machine
Wreaking havoc in our street
And tearing up the green
All those dirty shrubs have gone now
The carefully cultivated trees
Our flawed, imperfect, curated parkland
Ripped up, stripped out, thrown into destruction
Like some unsociable disease
Myopia is fine, if that's the way you like it
but fgs keep it to yourself
Stop insisting everyone starts wearing
Your dark black blinders for themselves
You shot my stallion and dared me not to flinch
I stared you out and would not give an inch
My knees caved in and buckled, I could not stand
Could not stand what you stand for
Missing all the juicy, nourishing, undergirding
subtext, foundation, fundaments
Replaced it all with simple surface, tarmac
"look how smooth we got it
with all that nasty foliage out of the way"
Your necessary tarmac
I stand again, brush myself down and look away

NEVER LOVED

You didn't answer every call I left
Didn't answer every question asked
Didn't always say just what you meant to say
Could I read your mind?
Maybe it seemed that way
Once upon a time

You didn't always look me in the eye
Didn't always speak your mind
Sometimes you kept for yourself
What should have been both yours and mine
If it meant so much, I didn't mind

So now I need to say this solitary thing
I never loved
It's as simple as this
I never loved you any less
For all of that

Keep it to yourself if it hurts to give away
But life is pain, sometimes
Come give it anyway
Be whole, be true and do what you need to do
I know you well, but sometimes
Even I still need a clue
Give me a cue and I'll come running

So now I need to say this solitary thing
I never loved
Oh, it's as simple as this
I never loved you any less
Never loved you any less

NIGHT OF THE LIVING DEADLINE

Not ready, full stop
Drop the options, create
New ones before I have a
Conniption, what do you mean?
I gave you all this time, a late
Very late deadline, five stitches
and you're done, in theory
But now I'm here, on time at
appointed hour but the project
Not just undone but not even
Started, what the heck?
Wasted so long to get this
When... what's that? Come back
in five minutes? No worries
See you then!

NO DOUBT (GOODBYE YESTERDAYS)

Severe? No, none of that here
Retry all misguided
Let go, that's all, don't hold so hard
Relax, unattach
There, that's got to be better
No need to try, ill-advised go-getter
What kind of perverse severance is this?
No attempt to move away
Away is where we are
No renegotiate is needed
You can't block your ears
Then accuse us of misreading
Falsely feeling, misperceived, unheeded
Now, not exactly that you are not invited
To come along this way as well
But the why of your arrival
Brings a sulphuric whiff of
Not hello, exactly
Not a skeleton key, exactly
How'd you get in here?
Persevered until the point of pain
Stepped aside to process, add it up
Disentangle, circumvent, prevent
No need to name names
To call it as it was is all
You knew just who and said it for yourself
One word could be recalled
But an attitude is not so clear to codify or modify
I thought your self-worn chains held back all you need
Right now your back is all I need to see

Go on, now, go away
Be free
Sail your paper boats across the puddles
Remaining of the water we passed
underneath that old bridge
Plus all your tears
So sad to see you, go
You're free now
Free of us
Free to do anything you want to do
We're no longer whispering critiques
At the back of the room
No longer bound by rules created
From your own self-doubts
No doubt about it
There is a little loss occurred
Don't try rebuild that shaky wooden bridge
So many matches in my pocket
We're over here already
Enjoying the sweet blaze
Of goodbye
Goodbye yesterdays

NOISIER

Was I white noise in your ear?
All of my attention
Just a little something
That you hoped would disappear?
'cos I'm sad, so sad if this were true
If all my murmurs of affection
Were just a bunch of noise to you

Was it a clanging of some gong
That made the fabric of our lives
Imagined togetherness
Now come undone
All my zipful conversation
Packed and shipped out
For another destination

Tweak the noise
Tweak the noise
Until it comes in tune

Twist your ears
Until you hear
That this is music
This sweet music
Is not just noise
Not just noise

Tweak the noise
Tweak the noise
Until it comes in tune
Until it all comes into tune

NOTHING IRONIC

Today we present to you
with no sarcasm
no cynicism
implied criticism The simplest sentiments
that we can find
no Gordian knots
No tricks to unwind

We LOVE YOU!
Thanks so much
For listening this far
We LOVE YOU!
Tune in for our other tunes on iTunes
View a bit more on Youtube
Look up a bit of it on Spotify
Throw us a couple of bob via Bandcamp
So, ta so much, we love you!

NOTHING LEFT

I got nothing left
You can take the rest
If all remaining functions stay the same
For every fading heart
For all that falls apart
Just keep it for yourself
I'll keep the blame

If all you ever wanted
Was a little piece
I hope this little sliver is enough

       Take it all
       There's nothing left
       Take it all
       Nothing remains

I got nothing left
You can take the rest
Come, sweep up
the ashes that remain
Phoenix has not arrived
No firebird in the sky
No gryphon
to ignite the dance again

All you wanted was a little peace
I hope this little moment is enough

       Take it all
       There's nothing left
       Take it all
       Nothing remains

Come, take it all
There's nothing left
Take it all
Nothing remains

Glowing scraps upon the breeze
Embers drifting through the trees
The biggest fires arise
From less than this

Glowing scraps upon the breeze
  (I give you everything I lack)
Embers drifting through the trees
  (Can't give what I no longer have)
The biggest fires arise
From less than this

Sometimes to clear
Your heart and mind
The little something left
Needs to
Be left
Behind

NUMB

Keep me away from all
that does not love me
Lock me in soft bandages
Plug my ears I never hear
A nasty word said of me

ON MY MIND

If you only had one thing to say
Would you guard it like some secret treasure
Or put that one thought on display
For me to read it, now or never

Oh say, say what's on your mind
Oh say, say what's on your mind

If you're allowed one thing to say
Would you spend it like some diamond moment
Measure twice, cut to the chase
Say it with your heart wide open

Come on, say what's on your mind
Come on, if you are so inclined
Maybe I want to know what's on your mind
Hmmm, I want to know what's on your mind

Do you mean it?
Do you mean it?
Is there something that you're feeling?
I can't read your thoughts from here
Do you mean it?
Do you mean it?
Is there something that you're feeling?
Speak aloud and make it clear
Oh say
Say what's on your mind
Oh say
Say what's on your mind

ONLY REMEMBER

If I could find it
I know I put it down
It's near here... somewhere
I'll see it in a minute

Whatever it was
If only I'd remember
I need it now I need it now
Whatever it was

Some things are just a loss
Some things merely misplaced
When I recover what I miss
All things will be in their right place

It's on the tip of my tongue
It's edging on my thinking
A hair away from my awareness
For now it's nothing giving me this distress

Whatever it was
If only I'd remember
I only know I need it now
Whatever it was

OTHERWISE

I used to see a falling star 'most every night
And think of you
See a promise slowly falling from the sky
And think of you
But time, time has shown it otherwise
Still all the falling skies
Must crash and burn somewhere

Time tears the heavens from the stars
So wherever you are
My lonely fallen star
I hope you're otherwise
Than lonely
Where you are

I used to seek the starlight
Glisten in your eyes
A promise sparkling
Gentle heaven
In your eyes
But time, time has shown it otherwise
Still all the falling skies
Must crash and burn somewhere

Otherwise we'd find the things
We'd sought so long
Otherwise all would be right with the world
Instead of wrong
Otherwise we'd open up our eyes
And see
The horizon isn't all that far
For you and me

OXYGEN

Would the world stop all its turning
If I just stopped all my walking
Would the cogs inside the big machine
Stop all their functioning

Would the world start sliding backwards
If I just stepped off the treadmill
Would we lose all of our balance
If I took a chance to catch my breath

Sometimes, sometimes I need to breathe
Sometimes I need to breathe the air
Inhale the clarity beyond the fog that's in my eyes and ears

Would the world stop all its spinning
If I took a moment at the beginning
To cease from all my labours
To desist from my frustrations
To abstain from my deflections
To absorb what once were redirections
To be still in the eye of whirling winds
Would all that spins slow slowly down
To nothings?

I breathe, I breathe the air
Inhale the clarity, that's fair

The rain will come
and after, that, sunshine, sometimes
And more or less rain
Who do you call for choreography in that situation?

I breathe, I breathe
I stop and drink it in

PLUS

To the plus
Just add it up
One plus one plus all begun
A snowball down a steep, steep hill
Could stop it anytime you want, but still
To learn, to grow, to theorise and know
To change and become more
Than what we started
Forget the friction of the earth
The scratches, wounds and scars are ours
So who would trade them off against the fun
A tumbling, turning snowball
Gaining all that extra skin
Don't second guess the grow
Just let it run

POEM ON DEMAND

A poem then, upon request
A boon for endless asking
Delivered best, beyond the jest
A project, job or tasking
Deliberation over words
Consideration, nouns and verbs
Can verse spring forth upon demand?
The proof, this poem, is in your hand
10.27pm commence
All done in three minutes
This ain't a bad show for it
Except for the last bit
Innit?

REMEMBERING

There's something about you I remember
If I could mark the place or find the time
But for now I'm just stirring up the dust
In the attics of my mind

All the little things you did
I remember that you did them
What were they now?
All the little pieces fade with time
What were they now?
Just fragments of remembering are left
The marks of memory
Faded, scorched and bleached away with time

All the memory I remember
There were memories and bliss
If I could I would remember you just like this

So far gone, what's still remaining
Simple shells and shadows of what was
Can I build another castle
From the sentimental debris
What would such a castle keep keep?
What would such a stronghold withstand
And would it stand beyond today?

All the deep remembering we made
Not all forgotten, but now faded
Not simply black and white
But deeply shaded
Little jewels that remain
Reflect the sunlight just the same

[ZERO]

ad astra: to the stars

REMIND ME

Mindful as I try to be
This isn't all it ought to be
And if sometimes
Something is out of line

Speak a little
Speak a little
Softly
Remind me

Secure to you as all I seek
Gentle, kind and sometimes meek
Strong where strong is needed
Mostly
Backed up to the bone
I will not leave you all alone

Speak a little
Speak a little
Softly
Remind me
What you need

And if the art of observation
Gives naught to contemplation
Nor resolves the situation
Or cools the mounting conflagration
Come bring the calm
The calm of your
calm conversation

Speak a little
Speak a little
Softly
Remind me
Speak a little
Speak a little
Softly
Remind me
I already know
Who you are
Who you are to me

REVEAL

All that is mysterious will be made known
All that is hidden will be shown
All that's tainted, bruised and broken
Now washed and mended
Made like new

No more hiding, no more shame
All that's shattered - whole again
All the misty glass will be wiped clean
We will see!
The lost will be found again

In the twinkling of an eye
It all changes
It all changes
You will see

In the twinkling of an eye
It all changes
It all changes

All that's strange will be explained
All that's tangled will be plain
We will know, we will be known
Each tear now wiped away
Every wound now tended, bound and healed
Every shame now cleaned away

In the twinkling of an eye
It all changes
It all changes
You will see

SKY

A fall into the nothingness
A leap of faith into the abyss
Who knew that all this being reborn
Could feel like dying?
We stand apart if just for now
A nod, a shrug, a little sigh
God knows why we feel so far
Beneath the earth
When we ought be flying
If I could cast a line with all my might
And pull the stars down from the sky
Perhaps this would be easier
Than dealing with what's ailing you and I

SO IT'S HAPPY

So it's happy ever after, after all this time
All the happiness is yours
All the aftermath is mine
Don't need to know the reasons
Some things simply have their seasons
This is fine

There's a newness to your naming
But yet not the one I chose
A sign of someone else's claiming
Some other one's suppose
Did you lose our gentle joys
Misplace all that we had known
Yes I looked the other way
Waited for it all to be out of the way
Did not know you would be gone so far
And not be back again

Now there's nothing I can do
to make you change your mind
There are promises to keep
I'm walking miles 'cos I was asleep
when it counted
And I ask questions of myself that I
would never ask of you
Not now

So is this therapy for me, to write it all out like this
So many stolen moments and barely a stolen kiss
If I was a thief for your attention
Yet I never stole your heart
That you acknowledged
Yet I never stole your heart
That you acknowledged

When pushing comes to shoving now
You can keep the choice you made
I could see it, now I'll leave it
For the hopes and dreams displayed
Not mine to touch or know no more
It's time right now to close that door
Regrets, perhaps, maybe, for sure
So close but now so far

All the calls I never made
All the words I never said
Still I wrote them in a song
Isn't that enough?
These are questions I know I must never ask again
And you must never answer
Not now

SOMETHING NEW

Sometimes the lure of the novel
Irresistible as it is
Is not as high tidingly subtle
as the stay-right-here of same old shoes
We know what we know
The same old how it goes
With everything that remains
And nothing there to surprisingly cost
Nothing there to lose

Also nothing else to gain
The roping tide of same
Old same old same old sane
And sometimes the new
footwear that's there
Is not just big boy shoes
But what the hey, rebooting boots
A call to new adventure
Nothing gained if nothing ventured
Don't know, not sure
Quite what it is you're actually in for
Comfort zones and old cocoons
Are made to leave behind
Sometimes the need for new
is all there is, it's true
Maybe ok, maybe a step or two
The unknown is not old shoes
But wear them well
And wear them in
And may all be well for you

SOUND AND FURY (GRIND)

Under your breath
every muttering uttered
Hard and slow
vehemently shuttering
Every wrong been done
against the obvious
What should have been
Could have been
No-one has seen

You could sail a kite
with a wind like that
You could launch a yacht
win the cup right back
You could dry your washing
in moments
in that breeze
Your windmilling
has ground no grain
Served no purpose
won no gain
Just tangled all kinds of knots
But there is no grindstone
here
for your axe
Here's the best I've got:
A cup of tea.
Relax.

THE STEPS

One step forward
Two steps awkward
Three steps and I'm falling
Right behind my schedule
Trying to hit fast forward
My life still finds itself on rewind
Nevermind the inclination
Where did you go
Lost momentum
Frantic lack of balance, too slow

One step sideways
Two steps to the alleys, byways
Three into the unknown
Destinies beyond the brochures
Hidden vistas, secret pastures
Faster to the forward
Finders find, no need for rewind
Inclination neverminded
Going to the Go
Full momentum now
Just go

Moment, just a moment
One more moment and we'll step out of it
One more moment and
We'll stitch the skin of the thing
With precision sutures
One more moment and we'll close old wounds
And find the future waiting

THOSE WAVES

The waves of old tradition
Crash upon the shore
And rocks break into raindrops
Ocean fury shattered clean and moist
And cold upon the skin of all my
Wandering, my wondering
Will endless ocean chills release me still
Or bring me back for more

VOICE

All the things I could not tell you
Once upon a time
It doesn't matter anymore
Now I've forgotten
What they were for
Not even gone to myth
Just gone like vapour, mist

All the things I would have yelled
From dusty rooftops in the past
Now signify to nothing
But the things that could not last
I would tell
Tell it all
But I've no voice for it
I have no voice for it
No voice for it anymore

WAIT

Are you waiting
Are you waiting
For that moment to arrive
When the world spins on it's axis
When the blur comes into focus

Are you waiting
Are you waiting
For that moment to arrive
Is your vision getting misty
Is it something in your eye?
Just let it out and if it's tearful
Let be joyful and not fearful
Let it shine

WELL

Can you hear me well?
Can you hear me?
Well, well, well

You made a change in my disposition
Through no argument or exposition
I absorbed the subtle glow
From the you I came to know

Every thought of you
Every thought of you
Has made me well, well, well
Every thought of you
Has made me well

WHAT WE KNEW

Any then, ever when
I never did make sense
of you, you knew it
Every word a see touch taste
Once a whirl, oh what a waste
It was a once upon another time
Did we make it rhyme?

If we could rediscover
All the rhymes of other days
Could all of our todays
Make new sense?

Anyhoo, everwoo
Needed to restart again
Crank the motor, stir the rotor
Dressed up like an absent voter
Speak or hold your peace, oh please
Another once, what is the time?
Does it have to rhyme?

WHAT WE KNEW NOW

I could write all kinds of letters
I could swear some affidavits
We could pledge all our endorsements
Fulfill our obligations

But if we could know right then
What we knew now
Oh-oh

We could set up some nice boundaries
We could build some taller fences
Paint them white and plant a lawn
Pretend we've come to all our senses
Against all accusations
we're needing no defence, this time
Don't ask what we don't know
Where could we look to find
Just what we need to show you now

If we could know right then
What we knew now
If we could know right then
What we knew now
Oh-oh

WINTER'S GONE

September, all these sunny days
Wild winds wend their ways
Let the Spring unfold

November, ending as you do
Turn a page or two
And we will find
Summer opens up her eyes
December comes as no surprise

It's shining
I'm just so glad it's shining now
Winter's leaving
Winter's gone

And if it's cold at night
Time will turn it out alright
Just wait and see
Just wait and see
Will Winter never lose its hold
Will that dark frost loosen its grip
On you and me, on you and me?

It's shining
I'm just so glad it's shining now
Autumn's leaving
Winter's gone

January
Well and wakened now
For all to see
All the hope
That hope can be
Shine your sun on me

THE WORLD AS WE DIDN'T KNOW IT

Today, today, my favourite day
Apart from any other day
I might have liked before
Today it's time to make it all shine
I'm fine now, I'm so fine
Now is the time

Is there one new thing
To think about a little
To grasp and gasp and get on with
So in my little old world
today begins
With a cheer of surprise
A scream of recognition
A click a go ignition in my brain

Ah! Hello to today
It's what I've got to work with
I'm so pleased you're here
If you have some hours to spend please stay
Ah today welcome, today
All I need right now
Is just begin today

Come on and let the day begin
Sun is shining let it never end
All it takes is something new
To think about a little bit
To grasp and gasp and get on with
So what in my little old world today
Begins with a cheer of surprise
And a scream of recognition
Ignition in my brain

VESPERS: GOOD EVENING

Thank you and God keep you
Safe until we meet
Again, beneath the stars
Or the clocks at Flinders Street
If one more cup of coffee
Is required before we go
Perhaps it's time, instead, for tea
So we can sit awhile
Chat, unpack, debrief, decompress
Undepress, enlighten, lighten
Float away in just the way
Only true companions on the way
Can comprehend
Or understand
Begin again
I'll wait
And see you then

THANKS

Of course, none of this is real. Except it's completely real.
I hope you don't believe a word
except that you feel it deeply, find something to relate to
and believe in the many words together.
Laugh and ponder.
It's fiction but real life too.
Some of it is me
some of it friends and friends of friends
some of it speculation, pure and simple.

To my thinking, poetry doesn't bring anything new to the
table, it just shows you what you already know.
What you knew that you knew, but hadn't quite
remembered that you did. New light through old windows.
Same house, seen afresh.

If you are someone I know or have known, or not, I hope
you find something of yourself in these pages.

May the words in this collection be as meaningful for you to
read, respond to, digest as they have been for me to write,
collate and publish.

Many thanks for encouragement, critique, inspiration and
friendship on the journey - Annie, Brian, Craig, Kristel,
Howie and Beth, Jono and Al, Justin, Kevin and Jan, Mike
and Jane, Leo, Steve, Vic, Wes and all the you-know-who-
you-are people I haven't named, whether for modesty or
amnesia.

Many thanks to my family.

Watch for more collections coming soon!

ABOUT THE AUTHOR

Martin Fawkes' love of word play began at an early age. "I remember writing poems in primary school, and the teacher calling my parents in to chat about them, like I'd done something really good, which I never quite believed".

Over time, however, it dawned on him this word play might be worth pursuing. Subsequent years in rock bands meant lots of songwriting, honing his poetry and storytelling skills into musical form.

Spoken word gigs followed, as did chapbooks and self-published collections of poetry and lyrics.

Now, many years later, here we are, published properly, at last. You hold in your hands part one of a four part sequence, celebrating a lifetime of writing.

- **Worlds We Leave Behind** (recent works)
- **Love, Devotion, Surrender and other bright ideas** (early 2000's)
- **To Cut a Long Story Short** (early works)
- **Surprise Visitors and other stories: the Christmas poems**

Milton Keynes UK
Ingram Content Group UK Ltd.
UKHW020741190124
436321UK00015B/682

9 780645 641905